HOPE & HEALING SERIES

WHEN YOUR CHILD LOSES A LOVED ONE

THERESA M. HUNTLEY

D1413776

MINNEAPOLIS

*Dedicated to my parents—Jim and Louise Jacobs
—who have always encouraged me to pursue my
dreams. Their love, support, and encouragement
have helped me to become the person I am today.*

Other books in the Hope and Healing series:
When Your Child Dies   *When Your Spouse Dies*
When Your Parent Dies   *When Your Friend Dies*
When Your Baby Dies through Miscarriage or Stillbirth

WHEN YOUR CHILD LOSES A LOVED ONE

Copyright © 2001 Augsburg Fortress. All rights reserved. Except for brief quotations in critical articles or reviews, no part of this book may be reproduced in any manner without prior written permission from the publisher. Write to: Permissions, Augsburg Fortress, Box 1209, Minneapolis, MN 55440.

Large-quantity purchases or custom editions of this book are available at a discount from the publisher. For more information, contact the sales department at Augsburg Fortress, Publishers, 1-800-328-4648, or write to: Sales Director, Augsburg Fortress, Publishers, P.O. Box 1209, Minneapolis, MN 55440-1209.

Cover design by David Meyer; cover art from Stone
Book design by Michelle L. N. Cook

Library of Congress Cataloging-in-Publication Data
Huntley, Theresa, 1961-
   When your child loses a loved one / Theresa M. Huntley.
   p.cm.
   Includes bibliographical references.
   ISBN 0-8066-4262-9 (alk. paper)
   1. Grief in children. 2. Bereavement in children. 3. Children and death. 4. Loss (Psychology) in children. 5. Children—Counseling of. I. Title.
BF723.G75 H86 2001
155.9'37'083—dc21   2001033768

The paper used in this publication meets the minimum requirements of American National Standard for Information Sciences—Permanence of Paper for Printed Library Materials, ANSI Z329.48-1984. ♾ ™

Manufactured in the U.S.A.   AF 9-4262

05   04   03   02   01   2   3   4   5   6   7   8   9   10

CONTENTS

INTRODUCTION

Someone has died and your child needs help. Where do you begin?

Let me start by saying I'm sorry for your loss. I'd like to commend you for reading this book. The fact that you are speaks to your commitment to help your child grieve. My hope is that you both will learn to live with the loss and embrace the meaning it will have for your lives.

As parents we may try to protect our children from painful things. When one thinks of death, there is a tendency to view it as a subject best avoided if possible. Even if this was your thinking before the death, you now realize there comes a time we must face that which is difficult.

A death has occurred and you have a choice. You can face the grief and begin a journey upon which you integrate the death into your lives or you can avoid the pain and bury it deep within. In reading this book you have chosen the former. I will offer guidance to assist you and your child on your grief journey.

🦋

As you begin this journey, reflect on your thoughts and feelings related to death. You may have experienced the death of a number of people in your life previously. Or this may be the first significant death you have faced. Whatever the case, if you are to be helpful to your child, self-awareness is critical. Consider what you think of death in general, as well as how you view your own mortality. Is death something that you fear? Does it have an element of mystery that holds some intrigue? Is it a part of the life cycle with a beginning as well as an end, both of which are accepted as part of the natural order of things? Ponder these questions and become familiar with your thoughts and feelings.

Children are naturally curious about life. If we have reflected, we are better prepared to address children's questions openly and honestly. On the other hand, if we are unaware of our feelings, we will be unprepared to answer the questions and to deal with the feelings that arise when we are confronted with them. Children are astute. They can often "read" our verbal communication, as well as that which is unspoken. Although we may be saying one thing, our nonverbal communication may be sending a contradictory message. Children will pick up on this and become confused. They may decide it's not okay to seek assistance from you.

🦋

It will be important to take special care of yourself during this difficult time. In helping your child face his or her grief, you are also making a commitment to deal with your own. You are on this journey together.

Consider how you have coped with difficult experiences in the past. What was helpful and what was not? Draw upon previous strengths. In doing this, you will be better equipped to meet the needs of your child. You will also be modeling the importance of self-care.

❧

This book is written to offer guidance as you assist your child in his or her grieving. It can be read from beginning to end, or you can choose a chapter at a time. The book provides information about how children understand death, as well as how you can talk about it with them. Ways in which children grieve will be discussed, as well as how to help your child in this process. As a means of illustrating the material, I will share stories drawn from my experience as a nurse and a social worker during the past fifteen years. To protect the identities of people involved, names and circumstances have been changed. For ease in reading, I have chosen to reference the child as a female. There is no intention on my part to suggest that one gender is more or less important than the other in assuming a female child.

Be gentle with yourself and your child as you begin this grief journey.

CHAPTER 1

HOW CHILDREN UNDERSTAND DEATH

In this chapter, I will discuss how children understand death, particularly from a developmental perspective. It is intended to provide you with an overview so that you have a general sense of what your child might be thinking.

Children gradually develop a concept of death directly related to their age. Their understanding is, of course, also influenced by other factors such as previous life experiences, emotional maturity, psychological development, coping abilities and style, culture and ethnicity, environment, and parental attitudes.

Specific patterns of thinking and behaving are unique to children at different stages in their development. Although many of these characteristics overlap, we can view these stages as five distinct groups based on levels of development: 1) children less than three years of age, 2) children three to six years of age, 3) children six to ten years of age, 4) children ten to twelve years of age, and

5) children twelve to eighteen years of age. These groups are approximations and should be used only as guides.

CHILDREN LESS THAN THREE YEARS OF AGE

Although children this age aren't able to understand the concept of death, they do respond to the experience of it in their lives. Infants and toddlers depend heavily on their parents. As a result, they worry most about separation. For them, dying means separation. (It is important to state that a grandparent or other adult may be the primary caretaker for a child. For the purpose of keeping this clear, however, I will use the word *parent* when referring to a child's primary caretaker.)

Infants have the task of differentiating themselves from the environment. They gradually develop a sense of being versus nonbeing. By approximately three months of age, healthy infants are secure enough to begin experimenting through games such as peekaboo with these contrasting states.

During the high-chair age, infants and children play games of disappear and return, dropping objects from their trays and waiting for someone to retrieve them. Children are delighted to have the objects reappear and will repeat the activity over and over again. With time, however, they begin to realize that not all things come back. Rather, they are "all gone."

As children begin to appreciate "all-goneness," they will continue to experiment with the concept through game playing. These can include such things as flushing objects down the toilet, blowing out a candle, or switching a light on and off repeatedly.

Although infants and toddlers do not understand what it means when someone dies, they do have a sense that something is different. They experience their care-givers as being distressed and are aware of the disruption this creates within their daily lives. It will be important for you to follow your child's routine as best you can. You will also find it helpful to be consistent in the expectations you have for your child's behavior. Routine and limits convey love and concern to children and it is critical that your child feel your love during this period. Finally, you want to provide basic information at a developmentally appropriate level, expanding upon this as your child grows older.

Children Three to Six Years of Age

Children in this age group view the world from the per-spective of their own experiences. Although they may use the words *die* and *dead*, they cannot truly compre-hend what they have not yet experienced. In addition, their vocabularies—although expanding—are also lim-ited. As a result, preschoolers rely on what they learn from their parents and other adults, their peers, their environment, books, television programs, and movies.

During this early phase in their development, children seem to regard death mainly as separation, a departure. It is clear to them that the dead are not here with us. For the preschooler, any separation or even the prospect of one—particularly from a parent—may be anxiety producing. These children may not be able to differentiate between what will be a short absence versus a long or permanent one. It is helpful, therefore, to tell children in terms they can relate to when you will be returning. You might, for example, say "Daddy will be home when it's time for dinner." In doing this, you are helping familiarize them with the numerous little separations that are a part of life.

Preschoolers believe death is reversible. For young children to understand the finality of death, they would need to be able to recognize themselves as capable of existing without their parents. This is beyond what they can imagine, so death is viewed as temporary. People may die, but they will come back.

Children this age also have difficulty imagining the nothingness of death. Although they may recognize that one's condition has changed, young children consider that the functions of the body continue. This is evidenced by the questions preschoolers ask. They want to know such things as: How will he eat and drink? Where will he go to the bathroom? Will he be able to breathe?

Magical thinking and fantasy reasoning are also characteristic of this age group. Young children are convinced of the power of their wishes. They believe their thoughts, words, or actions can cause a death. If, for example, a child wished a new baby sibling would go away, and then it does following a SIDS death, she will feel responsible. Or if the child yells at a parent during a fight, "I wish you were dead!" and the parent dies, the child may believe her words caused the death to happen.

Preschoolers may also view their actions, rather than the consequences of them, as being responsible for a death. They believe, for example, that if a person jumps into a pool and drowns, the death occurred because the person broke the rules about water safety. Death might also be considered as punishment for something they have thought, said, or done.

Children this age may also associate death with darkness, violence, evil, and sleeping. Nightmares and a fear of the dark can be common.

Children Six to Ten Years of Age

By the time a child enters school, many changes in thinking have occurred. These are the years of questioning. Early-school-age children gradually come to accept the idea that death is final, inevitable, universal, and personal. By age six or seven, they suspect their parents will die some day and the same fate *might* await them. They may accept the fact that a person has died and will not come back, but they do not yet fully grasp that everyone *must* die, themselves included. It's as if they need to find a compromise of sorts—a place that enables them to acknowledge the reality of death in general, while at the same time keeping it at a distance from their own life.

Although children in this age group are better able to test reality, magical thinking persists with the younger school-aged child continuing to overestimate the power of their wishes. Of more significance, however, is the strong tendency to personify death. Children view death as a taker, something bad that will come and get you and stop your life.

At this age, children begin to establish their own sense of moral judgment, contemplating right from wrong at a general level. They may continue to think of death as retribution for something they have thought, said, or done. These children may also try to reason out the meaning of life and death and to consider the possibility of an afterlife.

CHILDREN TEN TO TWELVE YEARS OF AGE

Children this age continue to develop their sense of what is right and wrong. Many will still consider death as a punishment for misdeeds. Although they are transitioning to a more adult understanding of the concept of death, they may still manifest remnants of magical thinking and fantasy reasoning.

Early adolescents are learning to understand both the biological process of death and the emotional aspects of it. At this point they are better able to comprehend the facts surrounding the death of someone than they are to understand the feelings. Unlike younger children, they now have a frame of reference and are intellectually able to handle much of the same information that is given to an adult.

Death at this age can be understood in relation to the laws of nature. In general, early adolescents may recognize that death is not an external power. Rather, it is an internal dysfunction within the body that causes life to end. These children will likely state the cause of death to be an illness, an accident, or old age.

Typically, early adolescents have moved beyond wondering what death is. They are now more focused on relationships and may ask questions such as, "What will happen to our family now that dad died? Who will take care of mom?" Concerned with practical issues, they may wonder if their financial situation has been impacted.

Children in this group have reached a turning point in their development. Given their increasing ability to think abstractly, they can now consider death in spiritual terms. Death is understood to be irreversible, universal, personal, and real.

CHILDREN TWELVE TO EIGHTEEN YEARS OF AGE

Adolescents hold many adult concepts of death and can cope with it in a similar manner. With well-developed cognitive skills, they intellectually understand that death is inevitable, irreversible, and universal.

As teenagers search for independence and meaning in life, they become focused on their bodies. They want to be accepted by their peers and be different than their parents. Teens tend to use friends as measures of success or failure in such things as family, school, physical and cognitive abilities, and social life.

Teenagers tend to be focused on the here and now. At the same time, however, they are beginning to think about the future. Thoughts become philosophical. They may consider "Who am I? What do I want to do with my life?" They may also ponder death and wonder, "If a person grows up to die, then what is the sense of life?"

Death is especially threatening to adolescents because it can destroy life and the body. It also illustrates that life can be interrupted and that goals can be destroyed.

Adolescents are faced with significant changes in their lives, many of which are beyond their control (i.e., puberty). People seek a certain degree of autonomy in life. When control is lost in one area, a person is likely to compensate by asserting control in another. For teens, thoughts of death or their own mortality may be too threatening or overwhelming. As a means of dealing with this, they may deny or defy death. Examples of this include such activities as speeding, experimenting with drugs, and engaging in unprotected sex with multiple partners.

CHAPTER 2

TALKING TO CHILDREN ABOUT DEATH

Children are naturally inquisitive about all aspects of life—and the cycle inherent within it—and will seek information in their attempts to gain an understanding of it. Ideally they will have a general knowledge of the concept of death before being faced with it on a very personal level. In any case, you need to ensure that discussions with your child include information about the basic facts of death, as these provide the foundation you build upon.

Before talking with your child about the death that has happened, give some thought to how you feel about death in general, as well as your own mortality. You will also want to reflect on the circumstances surrounding the death and the meaning it will have for you both.

Children are astute and can often "read" our non-verbal communication. If we are uncomfortable when we talk about death, we may unknowingly convey a message that death is something to be feared. Although our words may be saying one thing, nonverbally we may be sending a contradictory message.

When a death occurs, your child will have any number of questions that need to be explored and answered. These can range from questions that address the facts of the death itself (i.e., the cause of the death and the context in which it occurred), to those that deal with the matter of the body and what will happen to it. Children may consider what impact the death will have on their lives—both now and in the future. They may also wonder what the death might mean for other people. Children can have concerns about their own vulnerability and may be anxious they too will die. They may also mistakenly believe they might in some way be responsible for the death because of something they thought, said, or did. Certainly, we will be in a better position to respond to these questions and concerns in a helpful manner if we have pondered them beforehand.

TELLING YOUR CHILD ABOUT DEATH

Every situation involving death is different. Before discussing the death with your child, take time to consider the following:

What is the age and maturity level of your child?

What is your child's understanding of the meaning of the words died *and* dead?

Has your child experienced a death prior to now?

What is the relationship of your child with the deceased? How well did they know each other and how did they get along?

What are the circumstances surrounding the death?

What is your child's typical pattern of coping with difficult situations?

What are your family's religious, spiritual, and/or cultural beliefs about death?

The answers to these questions provide information about your child's understanding of death. Children gradually develop a concept of death that is directly related to their age, but which is influenced by other factors as well. The older or more mature child will have a more comprehensive understanding of death, as will the child whose life has previously been touched by it. In a situation in which the child and the deceased were emotionally close, feelings of grief will be more intense than if they were not significantly attached.

The nature of the death will have an influence on how your child deals with it. A death following a lingering illness is different than one that is sudden and related to a suicide or a traumatic incident. A death that was relatively peaceful is in sharp contrast to one that involves violence. If, for example, your parent has died after a prolonged illness, your child will likely have an awareness of the decline in health that ended in the death of her grandparent. To some extent this may have enabled her to anticipate the outcome and to begin to prepare for it (i.e., to say good-bye). A death that is sudden and unexpected typically does not allow for this. This is not to say that one situation is easier to deal with than another. It illustrates, rather, the point that the circumstances surrounding death are variable and it is important to understand what these differences can mean with regards to your child's grieving process.

The child's usual pattern of coping will also impact how she deals with the death. If your child tends to face life head on, it is likely she will similarly approach a situation involving death. If, however, she typically copes with difficult situations through denial or resistance, you can probably expect a similar response now.

Your family's religious, spiritual, and/or cultural views also need to be considered. The child whose family believes in life after death might be comforted by the thought of Grandma and Grandpa being reunited in heaven with God. The culture that embraces aging and death as a natural progression on one's journey may instill or promote a greater sense of understanding or acceptance of the death.

ESTABLISH RAPPORT
Open the Lines of Communication
When you are prepared to tell your child about the death, find a quiet, comfortable place that will allow

you and your child to talk freely without interruption. During this initial conversation, provide only the basic information. State simply who has died and what the circumstances were. If necessary, explain what the word *dead* means. Avoid overloading your child with too many details. The goal is to open the lines for further communication so that your child will feel comfortable asking for additional information later.

(It is important that your child have information regarding the death relatively soon after it has occurred. If time or other circumstances prohibit you from being able to do this, consider having someone who has a significant relationship with your child do this for you.)

Answer Truthfully

All children understand the experience of death at some level, so their questions regarding it must be answered truthfully and in words they can understand. Children seek a beginning, middle, and end to a story. If they sense that information is missing, they will fill in the gaps on their own. Often their imaginative answers will be far more disturbing than the truth itself. Children can be spared the terror of their imaginations if they are given truthful information in a simple, direct manner, as can be seen in the following example:

When Kathy, a seven-year-old girl, was told that her grandfather had been killed in a car accident, she was worried about what had happened to his body. Although Kathy knew her grandpa was dead, the thought of him being disfigured was disturbing. She asked her parents about the accident and the injuries that her grandfather had sustained, but they wouldn't talk about it because they worried it might be too frightening. When Kathy was able to view the body, she was relieved to see that her grandpa didn't look nearly as bad as she had feared.

By the same token, if you provide inconsistent answers, this can be confusing for your child and they may become anxious and unsettled. They may also determine intuitively that you are not someone whom they can rely upon for information in their grief process.

Answer Only What Is Being Asked

When answering your child's questions, be sure you understand what she is asking and provide only that information. Referring your child's questions back to her can clarify her specific concerns and inform you regarding what is bothering her. Oftentimes children will have an idea of the answer to their question in their heads, and they are seeking clarification regarding it. The following example illustrates the importance of understanding the question before you respond.

Peggy's big brother, Tom, died recently, and she has just asked you what will happen to his body now. You respond by asking, "What do you think, Peggy?" If she tells you something about Tom going to heaven where he will be able to play baseball all day, then you will have an idea of what she is thinking. You can respond appropriately, exploring her concept of heaven and sharing memories of

Tom playing baseball during his lifetime. Imagine how Peggy would have felt if you hadn't asked what she was thinking, and had gone instead into a detailed explanation about how the body is embalmed and then buried.

Encourage the Expression of Feelings

Convey to your child that it is all right to show her emotions. Let her know that whatever feelings she has are okay and that everyone expresses their emotions—even similar ones—differently.

Children look to their parents for guidance and will often model their behavior after them. If you openly share your feelings with your child, this will encourage her to do the same. It will also minimize the potential for miscommunication or misinterpretation that can result from keeping your feelings hidden from the child. The importance of sharing your feelings with your child is evidenced in the following example.

Jeff's mother has recently died following a short illness. Fortunately his dad talks openly with him about how much he misses Jeff's mom and how sad he feels without her. Jeff, in turn, talks about his sadness as well. If, on the other hand, Jeff rarely hears his dad talk about his feelings and he never sees his tears, Jeff might get the message that it's not okay to cry. He may even wonder if his dad loved his mom or if he misses her. Although Jeff's dad may cry in bed at night, if this expression of emotion is completely hidden from Jeff, it leaves him questioning his father and wondering what to do with his own emotions.

Accept the Feelings and Reactions Expressed by the Child

Avoid telling your child how they should feel and how they should act. Although there are many common feelings and reactions to a death, the grieving process for each child will be somewhat different. It is imperative that we recognize and respect this. Children in the same family can respond to the death of their parent differently as illustrated in the following example.

Five-year-old Matt and ten-year-old McKayla's mother has died following a long illness. Matt appears to be quite angry whereas McKayla talks freely about her sadness. When discussing this with the children, Matt tells you that he is mad at his mom for dying and leaving him. Not long before she died, Matt overheard his mother saying to his dad that she was at peace and prepared to die. Matt interpreted this to mean that his mother had chosen to die, which also meant leaving him behind. He is feeling abandoned and wonders who will take care of him now. McKayla understands that her mother was very ill and there was nothing more that could be done to make her better. Although McKayla is relieved that her mother will no longer be in pain, it is overwhelming to think of life without her loving presence and guidance. Both of these children's feelings are valid and need to be accepted.

It is also important to note that children's grief comes in waves. It is not uncommon, therefore, to experience them grieving in bursts—crying one

moment and then busily playing the next. This doesn't
mean they didn't love the deceased. Rather, it is a function of how children grieve.

Avoid Euphemisms and Confusing Explanations of Death

When talking with your child about death, avoid using
euphemisms. Euphemisms are less direct words or
phrases used to keep us from saying things we find dis-
tasteful. Avoid terms like *gone away, eternal rest, sleeping, passed on, lost, left us,* and *gone on a trip.* Instead, use
simple words like *dead* or *stopped breathing,* which convey the fact that the body is no longer physically alive.

As adults we can put euphemisms into context and
decipher their meaning. Children often cannot. Whereas
we may find comfort in the words, for the child they can
be quite confusing given the different meanings we
assign to them.

*Sam is three years old and his mom has just told him,
"We lost your grandma today." In Sam's mind this isn't a
big deal. He remembers getting lost at the store and being
found by his dad. All they have to do is go look for grandma
and and everything will be okay.*

*Mary is seven and has been told that her father was
"taken in his sleep." She is not, however, informed that her
dad had a heart attack. Mary becomes frightened and resists
going to bed at night, fearing she, too, could be "taken."*

Jessica's favorite uncle has died unexpectedly. Her par-

ents tell her he has gone away on a long trip and won't be able to visit anymore. Jessica is confused and hurt. Her uncle is very special to her and she questions why he would choose to go away and not come back. Jessica wonders if maybe she said something that made him not like her anymore.

INTEGRATE RELIGIOUS, SPIRITUAL, AND/OR CULTURAL BELIEFS INTO THE EXPLANATION

When discussing death with your child, be careful to share only information that is consistent with your religious, spiritual, and/or cultural beliefs regarding the soul, heaven, and life after death. Realize that what may be comforting to you as an adult, could be confusing and even frightening to your child.

It will be important for you to approach sharing your beliefs with your child similarly to how you approached the initial conversation about the death. Begin with the basics and lay a foundation of truth. Avoid making statements you may have to retract later. Be genuine in your explanation and consider how your words might be interpreted. If you share a concept that you have reservations about, your child will almost certainly detect your hesitation and become confused. They may also wonder about your truthfulness and be left questioning their own developing beliefs.

Terry's little brother, Billy, died recently of SIDS. Terry overheard you talking with a friend and heard her say, "God takes the angels to be with him" and "Now you

*have a guardian angel watching over you from heaven."
Although you may have found some comfort in these statements, Terry clearly did not. She is angry at a God that
would take her brother away from her. She is also worried
that if she is good, God might take her, too. As a result,
Terry begins to act out. In doing this, Terry is trying to
make sure God won't want her. She also is concerned
about being watched from heaven. Does that mean Billy
sees everything she does? Will he know if she plays in his
room and uses his toys?*

*Your father died a few days ago and today he was
buried. You attended the events with your husband and
four-year-old son, Danny. You are Catholic and, during
the funeral service, Danny heard the priest talk about
heaven. Having not heard this word before, Danny is now
asking you what heaven is. You explain that after a person
dies they go to heaven. Danny is quite confused, wondering how his grandpa could possibly be in heaven when he
saw his body buried in the ground earlier that day. You go
on to explain that although the body remains buried, it is
the soul that goes to heaven. Although Danny isn't quite
sure about this, you have given him some basic information and can expand on this in future conversations.*

CHAPTER 3

HOW CHILDREN GRIEVE

Grief is a process. It is experienced over time and becomes a part of one's life history. Children in particular will grieve and re-grieve a death throughout their lives as they grow, develop, and perceive the loss from new developmental perspectives.

As a means of understanding your child's grief, it will be helpful to have knowledge as to how it affects her physically, mentally, emotionally, and spiritually. Although your child's grieving will be an individual process—influenced by a number of factors—you'll likely note that she will exhibit many of the reactions described. Some will occur soon after the death, whereas others may be delayed. In helping your child, it is important that you accept your child's grief response as unique, taking care not to pass judgment or compare or contrast her reaction with that of another child.

Physical Symptoms

Linda Goldman, in her book *Life and Loss*, lists the physical symptoms many grieving children experience: fatigue, headaches, shortness of breath, dry mouth, dizziness, pounding heart, hot or cold flashes, heaviness of body, sensitive skin, empty feeling in body, tightness in chest, muscle weakness, tightness in throat, stomach aches, and increased illness.

Children who are grieving may experience physical symptoms similar to those of the deceased prior to their death. The cause of these symptoms can be multifaceted, and it will be important to explore them with your child so you can deal with them appropriately.

Children may express bodily distress because they are confused about what causes death, and they may be frightened that they, too, might die. If this is the case, ask your child what they know and think about death. Clarify any misconceptions they might have in terms that are understandable. If the death resulted from an illness, explain the difference between common, chronic, and acute illnesses. If an accident was involved, let them know it was a very serious one and the person's body was hurt so badly that it could no longer work right. With both illnesses and accidents, inform your child what you do to take care of both yourself and her so as to be as healthy and safe as possible.

Physical symptoms can also be your child's way of seeking additional attention. Reassure her that although this is a difficult time for everyone, you love her very much and will do your best to continue to give her the attention she needs.

THOUGHT PATTERNS

The thought patterns described in grieving children by Linda Goldman include inability to concentrate, difficulty making a decision, self-destructive thoughts, low self-image, preoccupation, confusion, and disbelief.

Bereaved children—like adults—may have difficulty paying attention or concentrating for any length of time. Explain that this is normal and in time it will be easier to focus. Reassure the child that you are aware it might be hard to concentrate on her schoolwork. Let her know you do not expect her to do as well right now. Inform the child's teachers of the death. This will prepare them for any possible behavior changes.

Grieving children—again, similar to adults—may find themselves thinking about the deceased all the time. It's as if there are constant reminders everywhere. These reminders may cause the children to experience unrelenting pain. In an attempt to find some relief, they may withdraw from the people and things that remind them of the deceased. Assure the child that this is normal, that you are all remembering the person who has died. Share your memories and talk about your feelings. Let your child know that you want to help her, emphasizing that running away from the situation will not make it go away.

EMOTIONAL RESPONSES

Feelings experienced by grieving children are listed by Linda Goldman as feeling unreal, anger, guilt, sadness, mood swings, depression, hysteria, relief, helplessness, fear, loneliness, anxiety, rage, and intense feelings.

It is common for children to experience denial of a death. Denial is a part of the grieving process. Death often comes as a surprise, and children—like adults—react in shock. Information that is painful may be pushed aside for a time. Upon hearing of a death, children will often resume play almost immediately. This does not mean they did not love the deceased or that they are unaffected by the death. Rather, denial provides a reprieve from the overwhelming sense of loss that often accompanies death. Just as adults need to take a break from the intensity, children do as well.

Bereaved children often feel angry about the death of someone close. This anger may stem from a feeling of helplessness or a loss of control, and typically it will be directed outwardly. Your child may, for example, be openly angry at the person who died for having left at a time when she needed them. This feeling can be intensified when they perceive the deceased as having had a choice in their death (i.e., suicide). Children may also direct their anger at others, such as God or the doctor, for not having saved their loved one. Children's anger can also be expressed less directly by acting out at school or home. Either way, it is important that you understand and accept this anger for what it is. Reassure your child that it is okay to be mad and encourage her to find appropriate ways of venting her anger.

At times children who are grieving may turn their anger inward, blaming themselves for the death. Your child may believe something she said, thought, or did somehow caused the death. Explore your child's feelings with her, listening for any misconceptions that require clarification. Review the cause of the death, emphasizing that something in the person's body was not working right because of an illness or injury. Reassure her that she is not responsible for the death.

Children tend to be self-oriented. Thus, when a death occurs and the structure of their lives change, it is not uncommon for them to worry about how their needs will be met. This is especially true when the deceased is a parent. (These children will frequently be heard asking the surviving parent, "Who will take care of me when you die?") Your child needs to know that you love her very much and that she will always be taken care of. Talk with her about all the people who love her and identify who would be responsible for her in the unfortunate event that you were to die. Emphasize that you hope to live for a long time.

COMMON BEHAVIOR CHANGES

The feelings of grief—together with one's thoughts—influence the behaviors that are seen in children who are grieving. Linda Goldman also lists these: sleeplessness, loss of appetite, poor grades, crying, nightmares, dreams of the deceased, sighing, listlessness, absent-mindedness, overactivity, social withdrawal, verbal attacks, fighting, extreme quietness, bed-wetting, clinging, excessive touching, and excessive hugging.

Grieving children may become overactive, searching aimlessly for something to do and jumping from one activity to another without an obvious purpose. They may also talk or giggle incessantly as they attempt to cope.

Bereaved children may withdraw from the people they love, afraid they too might die. They may also avoid getting to know new people because they are concerned about being hurt again. Reassure your child that you hope to live for a very long time. Acknowledge that although there is always the possibility that someone we love may die sooner than expected, being able to know and love the person makes it worth the risk. Communicate your love for your child and try to help her see that by withdrawing from other people she is cutting herself off from support at a time when it is desperately needed.

The death of a loved one often causes significant changes in a child's routine. The security of their daily life has been disrupted, and they may be overwhelmed. Lacking an adult's ability to cope, they may regress to earlier behaviors (i.e., bed-wetting, imaginary friend, increased independence on adults). In light of this, it will be important for you to try to follow her normal routine as closely as possible in an effort to restore a sense of order or security. You will also want to avoid making any unnecessary changes that could increase your child's stress and further disrupt her life.

Many children will become tearful and clingy when they anticipate a separation. Now that they have experienced a death—and have some understanding of the implications of it for their lives—they have a concern that other loved ones might also die. Acknowledge your child's anxiety and try to reduce it by preparing her for those times when you will be separated. Explain where you are going, whom you will be with, what you will be doing, and when you will be back in terms she will understand.

Bereaved children may try to replace the deceased by seeking the attention of another person. Tell your child that everyone will miss the person who has died and that it will be difficult to live without him or her. Reassure your child that although no one can ever take the place of the deceased, there will be other people to love.

At times children may assume certain mannerisms of the deceased and begin acting or talking like that person. Remind your child that you love her for who she is. Emphasize that although she may have some of the characteristics of the deceased, she is special and unique in her own right.

Children who are grieving may also remember only the good things about the person who has died. While it is comforting to remember these points, it is not healthy for your child to fantasize that the deceased was perfect or to deny any memories that contradict this. If you allow your child to idealize the person who has died, she may have unrealistic expectations of other people and herself by comparison. Emphasize that no one—not even the deceased—is perfect, but that does not prevent us from loving him or her anyway.

SPIRITUAL RESPONSES

When considering how your child experiences grief spiritually, it is important to draw a distinction between religion and spirituality. Religion is the organized or formal expression of one's beliefs that is shared in a faith community. Spirituality is comprised of your deepest personal beliefs. It serves to provide meaning for your life and connects you with a faith system or higher power of some kind. When people experience the death of a significant person in their life, it is not uncommon for them to find themselves in a period of profound questioning—a time in which they may struggle deeply with previously held beliefs.

Children tend to experience their spiritual questioning as a disruption in their sense of security, stability, predictability, and fairness in life. Their world has often been turned upside down, leaving them wondering what to expect and who or what to depend upon. They have experienced that bad things can in fact happen and that life isn't always fair. Ideally, grieving children—and adults as well—will be able to define or create some meaning for the death, and it will become integrated into their lives. In this process, their original beliefs will either be affirmed and strengthened or adjusted in some way.

In closing, it is important to note that in some cases bereaved children may be unable to grieve the loss when it happens. This could be due to a number of factors, such as their age or the support that is available to them at the time of the death. Whatever the reason, if children do not deal effectively with their feelings related to the death, they will not simply go away with time. At some point in the future, something will trigger these children's emotions, and they will be confronted with the grief that had been repressed earlier.

CHAPTER 4

TASKS OF GRIEVING

Because grief is a process, a number of grief educators have proposed that it has stages or phases. Others have associated tasks with grief, suggesting that these tasks not only comprise the work of grief, but also offer a means of understanding it.

Many people know of the pioneering work of Dr. Elisabeth Kubler-Ross. Through her work with dying people, Kubler-Ross recognized that there appeared to be "stages" that were experienced by these patients. The public responded to these stages quite literally and assumed people who were dying would pass through them sequentially. This general misinterpretation of Kubler-Ross's work is unfortunate in that it conflicts with the current perspective of grief as an ongoing process. Despite the general public's misperception of her important work, Kubler-Ross was clear to indicate that not only could dying individuals move through the proposed stages in varying order, they might also experience them more than once or not at all.

In *Good Grief: Helping Groups of Children When a Friend Dies*, Sandra Fox states that for grieving children to make their grief "good grief" they must accomplish three tasks: 1) understanding, 2) grieving, and 3) commemorating. J. William Worden, author of *Grief Counseling and Grief Therapy*, proposes that mourning requires the accomplishment of four tasks: 1) to accept the reality of the loss, 2) to work through to the pain of grief, 3) to adjust to an environment in which the deceased is missing, and 4) to emotionally relocate the deceased and move on with life.

In considering the experience of grief, I find the work of both Fox and Worden to be useful as a way of understanding it. Both of their first two tasks are similar and will, therefore, be presented together.

UNDERSTANDING: ACCEPT REALITY OF LOSS

To understand the death requires the children to know the person is dead and will never again return to be a part of their lives. To achieve this task, children need access to honest information in terms they can understand.

Initially you'll want to inform your child of the death with a simple explanation. Tell her the basic facts of the death itself and include a clear description about what the word *dead* means. Let her know that you are available to answer any questions she might have, as well as providing her with an opportunity to express whatever feelings she is experiencing.

Your child will likely think about this initial explanation and then seek out additional details as she is ready for them. Answer the questions she asks, providing honest information. This will lay a foundation of truth that you can build upon over time.

It is important to note that coming to an acceptance takes time. This, Worden states, is because it involves not only an intellectual acceptance, but an emotional one as well. Participation in traditional rituals such as the funeral can help a person to move toward acceptance.

GRIEVING: WORK THROUGH THE PAIN

Grieving involves working through the various feelings that are a part of mourning. Although adults and children mourn in similar, predictable ways, it is important to recognize within this the uniqueness of the experience for each individual. Just as the relationship between the deceased was unique, so, too, is the loss.

Whenever someone we have a deep attachment to dies, we experience pain. Although the intensity and expression of this pain may vary, the fact of its presence does not. It is necessary to work through this pain in order to grieve effectively. If the pain is avoided, it will remain until is has been addressed properly.

Various formal rituals (i.e., reviewal, funeral, memorial service) can help children channel their grief appropriately. When planning for these, it will be important to consider the needs of the children. The observances tend to be geared to the adult's expression of grief. Children can, therefore, be overlooked.

Participation in these rituals can facilitate the accomplishment of both tasks one and two as proposed by Fox and Worden. Not only can it move children toward an acceptance of the death, but participation will also assist them in experiencing the emotional aspects of it. It has been my experience that children usually want to be included in the family's grieving. More often than not, they choose to participate if they are engaged in a manner that is honest and encouraging.

Ideally, each child will be allowed—and encouraged—to participate at whatever level they feel comfortable. Children should not feel pressured into doing something that isn't comfortable. Offer support to your child and provide her with options.

You may choose to schedule a private viewing with the child. This will ensure that children can, if they want, see and touch the body in the presence of people whom they love and trust. The funeral director can be available to answer your child's questions and discuss any concerns she might have. This enables you to understand what your child is thinking, while taking the pressure off you at a time when you may be overwhelmed and unable to respond adequately to your child's questions.

At the funeral, be sure to have an understanding adult on hand who can be available for your child. This person can be responsive to the needs of your child, answering her questions and providing support. This will allow you to participate in the service without having the full responsibility for the care of your child. If your child chooses not to attend the funeral, consider having it videotaped for future reference.

COMMEMORATING

To commemorate is to honor or keep alive the memory of someone or something. It can be formal or informal.

Formal commemoration can include such things as memorial services, tributes in a yearbook, or the establishment of a scholarship fund.

Ways to informally commemorate someone can include doing something tangible as a means of remembering the deceased. These can include: planting a rosebush as a reminder of Grandma, donating a deceased child's favorite book to the school library, or creating a scrapbook to give to the parent of a child.

ADJUST TO AN ENVIRONMENT IN WHICH THE DECEASED IS MISSING

Worden states that adjusting to a new environment means different things to different people, depending on what the relationship was with the deceased and the various roles the deceased played. It is not unusual for it to take time after the loss for the bereaved person to realize what it is like to live without the deceased.

The bereaved person may be faced with adjusting to: 1) the loss of the roles previously played by the deceased, 2) their own sense of self, and 3) one's sense of the world. It will be necessary for them to learn new roles, develop new skills, and face life with a new understanding of it. The following example illustrates the complex process involved with this task.

Karla is fourteen when her father dies suddenly. She was close to her dad and enjoyed having him participate in many aspects of her life. He used to help with her homework and often attended her track meets. Her dad was deeply spiritual and taught faith formation classes at their church.

When her dad died, Karla's life changed. Her mom used to be home with her and her younger brother, George. Now she has a job. This means Karla helps more around the house. She and George often come home to an empty house and are responsible for doing their homework and starting dinner. Karla continues to run track, but it's not as much fun anymore. Her faith has been challenged and she struggles to make sense of a God that would allow her father to die.

During the next few years, Karla learns to enjoy cooking and feels good about being able to help. She realizes that running is something she can do with her brother and convinces him to join the track team. They are seen together frequently at the track. Karla seeks guidance from a priest, wanting to believe again in a loving God.

Gradually Karla comes to accept that all people die. Although she may never understand why her father died when he did, Karla finds comfort in the belief that God shares her grief. She misses her dad's daily presence in her life, but carries his memory in her heart. As a tribute to him, she becomes a Sunday school teacher.

EMOTIONALLY RELOCATE THE DECEASED AND MOVE ON WITH LIFE

When a person dies, Worden states that people are faced with the task of finding an appropriate place for the dead in their emotional lives—one that will enable them to go on living effectively in the world. The thoughts and memories that one associates with the deceased will always remain with you. They must, however, be relocated over time in your emotional life if you are to move forward. If a person holds on to the past relationship, it can prevent her from being able to go on and develop new ones. The fact that one moves on and establishes new relationships does not in any way minimize the love that she had for the deceased. It signals, rather, that there are other people to love and she is ready to begin to live life again. The delicate balance between finding an appropriate place for the deceased in your life so as to be able to move forward with it is illustrated by the following example.

Peter was five when his little brother, John, died in a drowning accident. John had been just one year younger, and they had been the best of friends. They spent hours playing together and it was hard for both when Peter started school. John used to wait on the front steps each day, eagerly waiting for the bus that would bring his brother home.

On the day of the accident, they had been swimming at the community pool. Typically they were always together, but on this day they became separated. Somehow John had bumped his head and gone underwater unnoticed. Peter witnessed the attempts to resuscitate his brother and was devastated when his mom told him John had died. Peter couldn't believe that John was dead. Each day when he got off the bus he looked to see if John were there.

Gradually over the next few months, Peter began to realize that John wasn't coming back, just as his mom had said. He spent hours sitting in the room they had shared. Peter thought of all the fun things they had done together and became angry when he realized he and John would never play together again. His mother tried to get him to do things with some of his friends from school, but Peter wasn't interested. They weren't John.

In the midst of this, a new family moved next door. Peter's mom told him there were two girls and one boy. The boy, Tim, was five—just a little bit older than John would have been. At first Peter didn't want anything to do with Tim. It was too painful. It should have been he and John together that got to know Tim. But John wasn't here.

Peter's mom began to ask Tim to come for lunch on

Saturdays. Slowly Peter began to enjoy Tim's company and they started to play together after school. At first Peter felt strange about this. He wondered if it was okay to have fun again. Did it mean he didn't miss John, that he hadn't loved him enough?

Fortunately Peter and his mother had a good relationship. Peter was able to talk with her about most everything, and one day she asked him how it was to have a new friend. Peter confided that he felt sort of mixed up. He really liked Tim, and they had a lot of fun together. Peter still missed his brother, but he was discovering that he could be happy again. He asked his mom if this was okay or did it mean he didn't love John. His mom assured him that John would always be his brother and that he would always be with them in their hearts. She said they had all loved John very much and that they would never forget him.

Peter and his mom had talked openly about John after his death, sharing their memories and thinking about what he would be doing if he were there with them. His mom suggested that maybe it might be helpful to talk with Tim about his brother, to share some of his favorite stories about him. Peter began to do this and found that it was helpful to remember John in this way.

CHAPTER 5

HELPING CHILDREN GRIEVE

As adults, we may want to protect children from that which is painful. We have often heard someone say, "If only I could make it better for him" or "I would give anything to trade places with her." Life happens—and in it there is the potential for great joy and sadness. While we cannot change the fact that a death occurred, we can have a significant impact on a child's experience with it. Rather than remain passive about that which is beyond our control, it is helpful instead to focus on what we *can* do.

BE AWARE OF PERSONAL FEELINGS

When we are aware of our own feelings, we are in a better position to help bereaved children cope with theirs. Then we can work together toward the goal of integrating the death into our lives.

Before attempting to help your child, take time to reflect on your own feelings related to the death that has occurred, as well as your feelings regarding the fact that you will die someday. Children take their cues from adults—particularly their parents—and your ability to deal with the reality of the situation will influence your child's acceptance or denial of the death.

RECOGNIZE THAT EACH CHILD'S LEVEL OF UNDERSTANDING OF DEATH IS DIFFERENT, AS IS THEIR GRIEF RESPONSE

Remember that each child's understanding will vary according to such factors as age and developmental level. Provide your child with information and responses appropriate for her age level and needs. Then build upon this information as her understanding gradually develops.

Although many people may have similar feelings, the grief process is an individual experience. How children will grieve the death is influenced by the responses of those close to them, as well as by their relationship with the deceased.

ENCOURAGE QUESTIONS

When someone dies, children usually want to know what has already happened, as well as what will be happening now—and they have a right to this information.

Tell your child honestly what has occurred and explain, when necessary, what the word *dead* means. Let your child know you want to help her through this and are willing to talk with her openly about all aspects of the death, including her feelings related to it.

Reassure your child you will do your best to answer her questions. At the same time, however, do not be afraid to say, "I don't know." If your child senses she is being given honest information, she will feel comfortable talking with you about her experience with the death. Typically she will ask a few questions and then go away to think about what has been said. When your child is ready for more information, she will come back with additional questions.

If at any time you cannot deal with your child's questions (i.e., when you are physically or emotionally exhausted), tell her why you can't explain now. Next tell your child when you will get back to her to discuss her questions. If you neglect to do this, your child might think you are avoiding the issue or withholding information. This in turn may cause her to question both your integrity and your willingness to talk with her.

ENCOURAGE THE EXPRESSION OF FEELINGS

Let your child know that it is okay to show her emotions. Sharing your feelings with her is one of the most effective ways of encouraging expression of her feelings. As mentioned, children tend to look to their parents for guidance and will often model their behavior after them.

At times a parent will verbalize concern about letting their child see their sadness or anger. It has been my experience that allowing children to see our vulnerability plays an important part in helping the child's own grieving. Children need to know adults have feelings, too.

What is critical in this is not only the fact that we have the feelings, but just as importantly what we *do* with our feelings. If we demonstrate an ability to cope with them effectively, this conveys a sense of comfort or security to the child. On the other hand, if we become disabled by them and unable to function, this can be very frightening to a child. Given their dependence on us, children need to know that they will be taken care of, even in the face of grief.

Help your child realize that although everyone might have similar feelings, each will express them differently. By sharing your emotions openly and honestly, your child will be more likely to feel comfortable expressing her own. Fewer problems develop when children don't have to guess how others are feeling.

ENCOURAGE PARTICIPATION IN THE RITUALS

Spend time preparing your child for the events that take place during the days immediately following the death. Often what is most distressing for a bereaved child is not knowing what will be happening and how they will fit into the events. Outlining the events of the next few days could save your child from unnecessary anxiety and worry during what is already a very difficult time.

Tell your child about the events that will be taking place (i.e., reviewal, funeral, burial). Explain that these rituals provide us with a way to say good-bye to the deceased and to celebrate the life they lived. Answer any questions your child has about the rituals. Give her permission to choose how and to what extent she will participate in the activities. Emphasize to your child that she will not be forced to do anything that feels uncomfortable to her.

HELP THE CHILD COMMEMORATE

It is often beneficial to help children find a meaningful way to commemorate the life of the deceased. Share your favorite memories of the person with your child and invite her to do the same with you. If possible, offer your child a possession from the deceased that holds a special meaning for her. This could be a special CD from an older sibling, a fishing pole from a grandfather, or a favorite piece of jewelry from a mother.

Ask your child how she wants to remember her loved one who has died and then help her to find ways to do this. If, for example, Johnny and his grandpa spent a lot of time fishing, on the anniversary of the death you and your child could go back to a favorite fishing spot. Or if Emily and her grandmother used to enjoy picnics under a tree in grandma's yard, maybe Emily would like to plant a similar tree at her home. Assisting children with such a memorial will facilitate a healthy resolution of their grief.

TRY TO MAINTAIN A SENSE OF NORMALCY

Grieving children often experience their world as being in turmoil. To restore some semblance of security, try to follow your child's normal routine as closely as possible. This will bring some structure and stability to an environment that seems completely out of control.

If you are overwhelmed and unable to adequately care for your child, consider having someone familiar to her come to help you with her during this difficult time. This enables your child to be near you and to feel a part of what is happening, while relieving you of the full responsibility for her care. If you send your child away, she may feel her grief is unimportant because she is being excluded from sharing in the family's grief.

In the first few months following the death, try to avoid making any drastic changes (i.e., moving to a new home) unless it is absolutely necessary. These changes—as much as they might be beneficial to us or seem positive for the child—could increase a child's stress through additional change and loss, creating an added burden.

USE RESOURCES AND SEEK ASSISTANCE

When grieving the death of a loved one, we may feel completely overwhelmed, barely able to meet our own needs, much less provide adequately for those of our child. Express your needs and ask for the help you need.

Initially it may be helpful to have assistance with the details of the funeral or service. You may also have various offers to help with routine household tasks. Don't be afraid to accept these offers. People want to help and these activities provide them with a means for doing so.

As time goes on, your needs may change. Whereas in the past you required assistance with physical tasks, now you may want a friend to listen to the feelings you are experiencing as the emotional numbness subsides. Whatever the case, remember that just as you may need assistance in your grief work, so too may your child.

There are a number of resources available to help children in their grieving process. Their school, your church, or a local hospital may offer a children's grief support group. Participation in such a group provides children with an opportunity to learn more about grief, as well as ways to cope effectively with the feelings associated with it. In addition, when bereaved children get together they become aware that they are not alone in their grief. They learn other children have also experienced the death of someone close to them.

Local bookstores and libraries have numerous books that can prepare us for our interactions with grieving children. Some are designed to be read with your child. Others will be directed toward you as the adult. Still others are available for children to read independently.

The Internet also offers a way for accessing information. Not only will it give you material on the topic, it may also provide you with an opportunity for support through a chat room.

Finally, counselors who specialize in the area of grief can be helpful to you and your child. While certainly not all children will require individual counseling, there are cases when it does become necessary. The feelings of grief are initially very intense. If they are coped with effectively, however, the intensity will gradually ease. When the feelings remain intense for an extended period of time, additional intervention may be necessary.

If your child does not seem to be able to live with the loss—as evidenced by the continuing intensity of their feelings and reactions to the death over an extended time period—or if you have any questions or concerns, don't hesitate to call a trained professional. You could learn that your child is in fact grieving the death as one might expect and that you are doing what you can to facilitate a healthy grieving process. Or you might find that your child is having difficulties beyond what would be considered within the norm and intervention may be recommended. Either way you can rest easier knowing that help is available to you and your child. There are others to share the grief journey with you.

CHAPTER 6

LIVING WITH
THE DEATH DURING
A LIFETIME

The grieving process has been likened to waves of an ocean. Feelings of grief are natural, often experienced as an ebb and flow of emotion. We can choose to prepare ourselves to ride with the flow of the water or we can resist the driving force beneath it. In making this choice, consider that grief is not something that will simply go away with the passage of time. Even if buried deep within, the feelings will one day rise again to the surface and command our attention.

As you and your child grieve the loss and search for the meaning it has for your lives, you will find there are times when your grief is all consuming. In the days immediately following the death, this is almost certain to be your experience. As you move through some of the traditional rituals surrounding the death, you may begin to find this shifting a bit. Although you may continue to think of the deceased much of the day, there will be brief moments when you are able to focus on something else.

In the months following the death, you will continue to experience waves of grief. As you return to some of your routine activities, you may take a measure of comfort in the security these provide. Although the grief you carry remains, ideally it will become a part—rather than all—of you. In this process it will be important for you and your child to face the feelings that the death has brought forth. Be open in your discussions and freely share your memories.

When considering the question of whether mourning ends, know that there is no definitive answer. Having said this, I will say that there is a growing sense that it can take at least one year—if not two—to fully grieve the death of someone important to you. If you think of the year immediately following the death, consider the number of "firsts" it will hold (i.e., the birthday of the deceased, holidays, the anniversary of the death). It will be important for you to plan for these days, taking time to consider what you want to do and with whom you want to spend them.

When thinking of grief specifically as it involves children, it is important to note that they will grieve and re-grieve the death throughout the course of their lifetimes. Typically, normal developmental milestones in a child's life can trigger this process (i.e., the first day of school, graduation, getting married, becoming a parent). Acknowledge the significance of these milestones for your child and be aware of her need for increased support around them.

As you continue on this journey of grief with your child, know that you have embarked on what will be a lifelong process. Although you will undoubtedly encounter people who want you to "get over" your grief, you have likely realized that this is not the goal you are moving toward. Ultimately you and your child will learn to live with the loss and its implications for your lives. You will come to embrace the meaning of the death, weaving it carefully into the fabric of your lives. Just as the person who has died was a part of your lives, so too will be your memories of him or her.

Again, initially this may seem overwhelming, perhaps even inconceivable. You have been devastated and it's difficult to imagine life beyond the pain and intensity of the current moment. You will find, however, that the time will come when your sadness has lightened and memories of the deceased bring with them a gentle comfort. The waves of emotion—although continuing now and again to wash over you—do so less often and with decreased intensity. Life will one day hold new hopes and dreams for you and your child, and you will experience again the joy that these can bring forth.

WORKS CITED

Fox, Sandra, *Good Grief: Helping Groups of Children When a Friend Dies* (Boston: The New England Association for the Education of Young Children, 1999 [1985]). Copyright © 1984, 1999 New England Association for the Education of Young Children.

Goldman, Linda, copyright © 1994 from *Life & Loss: A Guide to Help Grieving Children* by Linda Goldman. Reproduced by permission of Taylor & Francis, Inc., http://www.routledge-ny.com.

Worden, William J., *Grief Counseling and Grief Therapy* (Springer Publishing Company, Inc., New York, NY 10012, 1991). Copyright © Springer Publishing Company, Inc. Used by permission.